P9-DZZ-775

New Hampshire

A Buddy Book
by
Julie Murray

ABDO
Publishing Company

VISIT US AT

www.abdopub.com

Published by ABDO Publishing Company, 4940 Viking Drive, Edina, Minnesota 55435.

Printed in the United States.

Edited by: Sarah Tieck
Contributing Editor: Michael P. Goecke
Graphic Design: Deb Coldiron, Maria Hosley
Image Research: Sarah Tieck
Photographs: AP/Wide World, Clipart.com, Comstock, Corbis, Digital Vision, Getty Images, Library of Congress, One Mile Up, Photodisc, Photos.com, William Johnson

Library of Congress Cataloging-in-Publication Data

Murray, Julie, 1969-
    New Hampshire / Julie Murray.
        p. cm. — (The United States)
    Includes bibliographical references and index.
    ISBN 1-59197-688-X
        1. New Hampshire—Juvenile literature. I. Title.

CURR F34.3.M87 2005 2006
      974.2—dc22

                                                    2005046949

Table Of Contents

A Snapshot Of New Hampshire

When people think of New Hampshire, they think of its history. It was one of the first states in the United States. Captain John Mason sent people to New Hampshire to establish a fishing colony. Mason named New Hampshire after his hometown in England.

Scenic New Hampshire.

There are 50 states in the United States. Every state is different. Every state has an official nickname. New Hampshire's nickname is the "Granite State." This is because granite is found throughout the state.

New Hampshire became the ninth state on June 21, 1788. Today, it is the 44th-largest state in the United States. It has 9,283 square miles (24,043 sq km) of land. New Hampshire is home to 1,235,786 people.

Many people live in the state of New Hampshire.

Where Is New Hampshire?

There are four parts of the United States. Each part is called a region. Each region is in a different area of the country. The United States Census Bureau says the four regions are the Northeast, the South, the Midwest, and the West.

New Hampshire is located in the Northeast region of the United States. New Hampshire has four seasons. The seasons are spring, summer, fall, and winter. Summers are mild, while winters are cold and snowy.

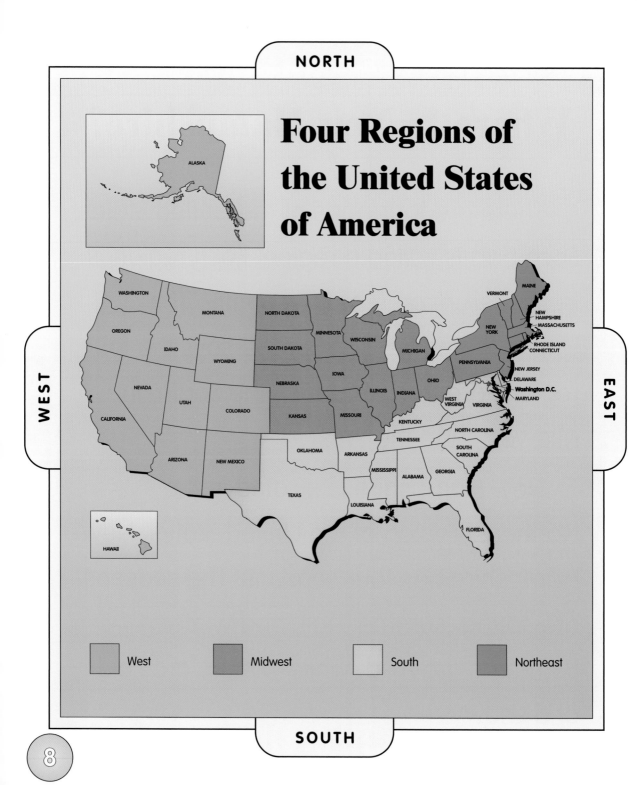

Four Regions of the United States of America

ALASKA

WASHINGTON

OREGON

MONTANA

IDAHO

NORTH DAKOTA

MINNESOTA

WISCONSIN

VERMONT

MAINE

NEW HAMPSHIRE

MASSACHUSETTS

NEW YORK

RHODE ISLAND

CONNECTICUT

WYOMING

SOUTH DAKOTA

MICHIGAN

PENNSYLVANIA

NEW JERSEY

DELAWARE

NEVADA

UTAH

COLORADO

NEBRASKA

IOWA

ILLINOIS

INDIANA

OHIO

WEST VIRGINIA

VIRGINIA

Washington D.C.

MARYLAND

CALIFORNIA

KANSAS

MISSOURI

KENTUCKY

TENNESSEE

NORTH CAROLINA

ARIZONA

NEW MEXICO

OKLAHOMA

ARKANSAS

MISSISSIPPI

ALABAMA

GEORGIA

SOUTH CAROLINA

TEXAS

LOUISIANA

FLORIDA

HAWAII

West Midwest South Northeast

New Hampshire shares its borders with three other states. It also borders a body of water and the country of Canada. Maine lies to the east. Massachusetts is to the south. Vermont borders the state to the west. Canada is to the north. The Atlantic Ocean is on the southeast corner.

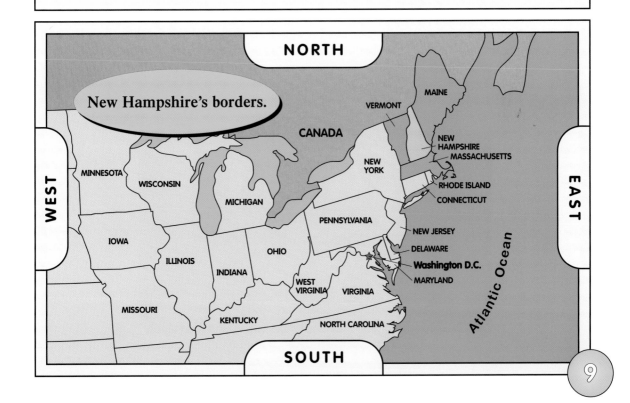

New Hampshire's borders.

New Hampshire

State abbreviation: NH

State nickname: Granite State

State capital: Concord

State motto: Live Free or Die

Statehood: June 21, 1788, ninth state

Population: 1,235,786, ranks 41st

State flag:
Adopted in 1909

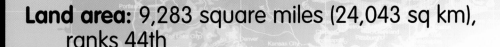

Land area: 9,283 square miles (24,043 sq km), ranks 44th

State song: "Old New Hampshire"

State government: Three branches: legislative, executive, and judicial

Average July temperature: 68°F (20°C)

Average January temperature: 19°F (-7°C)

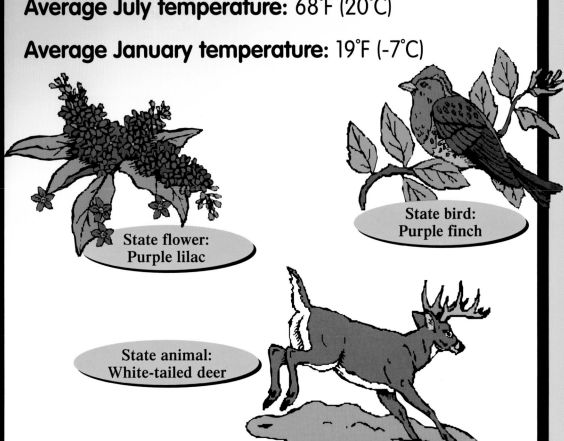

State flower:
Purple lilac

State bird:
Purple finch

State animal:
White-tailed deer

Cities And The Capital

Concord became the state capital in 1808. It is located in the south-central part of the state along the Merrimack River. Concord is home to the Museum of New Hampshire History. There, visitors can see exhibits and learn about the state's heritage and traditions.

New Hampshire State Capitol

The Merrimack River is in Concord.

Manchester is the largest city in New Hampshire. It is also located on the Merrimack River. The Amoskeag Mills in Manchester were once the largest textile mills in the world. During the American Civil War, these mills also made muskets.

A view of the Amoskeag
Mills yards in Manchester.

Many boats visit
Portsmouth Harbor.

Portsmouth is one of the oldest cities in New Hampshire. It is on the coast of the Atlantic Ocean. The city was first settled in 1630. At that time, it was named Strawberry Banke.

Famous Citizens

Christa McAuliffe (1948–1986)

Christa McAuliffe was a high school social studies teacher from Concord High School. She was to be the first civilian in space. McAuliffe was part of a special program. She was picked to go into space with six astronauts. They would fly into space on a space shuttle called *Challenger*. The *Challenger* exploded after liftoff. All were killed. This was a sad day for Americans. Today, people can visit the Christa McAuliffe Planetarium in Concord.

Christa McAuliffe

Famous Citizens

Franklin Pierce (1804–1869)

Franklin Pierce

Franklin Pierce was born in Hillsboro. He was the 14th president of the United States. Pierce served from 1853 to 1857. Pierce is the only United States president from New Hampshire. He was president during a very prosperous time. The United States was growing. People were moving west. Also, the gold rush was happening.

Famous Citizens

Earl Tupper (1907–1983)

Earl Tupper was born in Berlin. He invented Tupperware. These are well-known plastic storage containers. Today, the company makes $1.2 billion in yearly sales.

Earl Tupper invented Tupperware.

New Hampshire's Weather

New Hampshire has four seasons. Wildflowers fill the landscape in spring. Summers are short and cool. Trees turn vibrant shades of orange, red, and yellow during the fall. Winters are long and cold.

New Hampshire has some of the coldest temperatures ever recorded in the United States. It also has some of the country's strongest winds. These happen because of the Atlantic Ocean. The Atlantic Ocean borders New Hampshire.

New Hampshire's weather can be extreme.
It can get very cold and windy in the winter.

New Hampshire's Landscape

New Hampshire's landscape is hilly, rocky, and heavily wooded. More than 80 percent of New Hampshire's land is forest. There are beech, birch, elm, fir, hemlock, maple, oak, and pine trees.

There are about 1,300 lakes and ponds in New Hampshire. The largest is Lake Winnipesaukee. It is about 70 square miles (181 sq km).

A rushing river in New Hampshire.

New Hampshire is divided into three regions. The southeast region is known as the Coastal Lowlands. This is the area where New Hampshire borders the Atlantic Ocean. Sandy beaches line the coast. Thousands of birds stop there on the way south for the winter.

The largest cities are located in the New England Upland region. There are big cities, factories, mills, and farmland.

New Hampshire is known for
its rugged, rocky coastline.

The northern part of New Hampshire is the White Mountains Region. It consists of mountains and valleys. The highest point is Mount Washington. It stands 6,288 feet (1,917 m) tall. Some of the worst weather in the world has been recorded there.

The most famous area of the White Mountains is called Presidential Range. Each of the six peaks is named after a president.

Mount Washington is in
the Presidential Range.

New Hampshire

1614: Captain John Smith of England explores the Isles of Shoals.

1680: England establishes New Hampshire as a separate royal colony.

1776: New Hampshire becomes the first colony to declare independence from England.

1788: New Hampshire becomes the ninth state on June 21.

1833: One of the first United States public libraries is founded in Peterborough.

1890: University of New Hampshire admits its first two female students.

1916: New Hampshire holds its first primary.

1945: World War II German submarines known as U-boats surrender in Portsmouth.

1961: Alan B. Shepard Jr. of East Derry becomes the first American in space.

1996: Jeanne Shaheen is elected as New Hampshire's first female governor.

2003: A landmark known as Old Man of the Mountain crumbles to the ground.

Before

After

These two views show Old Man of the Mountain, before and after it broke off.

Cities In New Hampshire

Dixville Notch •

Berlin
•

Concord ★   Dover •

Hillsboro •   Portsmouth •

Keene •   Manchester •

                East Derry •

Peterborough •

Nashua

Important Words

American Civil War the United States war between the Northern and Southern states.

capital a city where government leaders meet.

civilian a person not in the military.

colony a settlement. Colonists are the people who live in a colony.

heritage a tradition or practice that is handed down from the past.

musket a gun used during the American Civil War.

nickname a name that describes something special about a person or a place.

textile having to do with cloth or fabric.

World War II the second war between many countries, which happened from 1939 to 1945.

Web Sites

To learn more about New Hampshire, visit ABDO Publishing Company on the World Wide Web. Web site links about New Hampshire are featured on our Book Links page. These links are routinely monitored and updated to provide the most current information available.

www.abdopub.com

Index